THE RED
D ◇ R ◇ U ◇ M

Jane Candia Coleman

Poetry of the American West

THE RED
D ◇ R ◇ U ◇ M

JANE CANDIA COLEMAN

HIGH PLAINS PRESS
GLENDO, WYOMING

Cover photo by Jane Candia Coleman.

FIRST PRINTING

1   3   5   7   9   8   6   4   2

Library of Congress Cataloging-in-Publication Data

Coleman, Jane Candia.
The red drum: poetry of the American west
Jane Candia Coleman.
p. cm.
ISBN 0-931271-28-2 (soft: acid free)
1. West (U.S.)--Poetry.
I. Title.
PS3553.047427R43   1994   94-36726
811'.54--dc20   CIP

HIGH PLAINS PRESS
539 CASSA ROAD
GLENDO, WY 82213

ACKNOWLEDGMENTS

The author gratefully acknowledges a grant from the Arizona commission on the Arts which enabled her to travel and gave her time to write many of the poems that follow.

Poems in this book have appeared in *The Critic, Concho River Review, Xanadu, Backcountry, Footwork, The Pittsburgh Quarterly, The Pittsburgh Center For the Arts Magazine,* and *Hyperion.*

C O N T E N T S

III. Beyond The Meridian

I

THE EDGE

OF YEARS

HIEROGLYPHS

FROM THIS HIGH up you were
the first to see the sun rise,
to watch the mountain rocks
turn crimson in the dawn.

A river flowed in the valley then.
It caught the light and hurled it,
brilliant fragments
from wind-rumpled mirror.

Now, standing in your place,
I know your ecstasy.
I know that driven by a need
you hardly understood
you dipped your fingers
into paint and, trembling, drew
the rising sun
ripples of water
a figure, arms stretched wide,
dancing on the edge of years.

By the Washita

THE REDBUD IS in bloom, Black Kettle.
The grass is green, high enough
to fatten all your ponies.

Tall grass, the river running high,
and blossoms bursting on the banks —
a loveliness, a terror,
a thousand broken hearts
dancing in the trees.

What is seen can deceive.
What is felt
may be only the self
filled with vain hope.

You took a flower in your hand
and dreamed;
forgot the sting.

The redbud is in bloom, Black Kettle.
The river flows.
And you and your Cheyennes,
the bones of all your ponies
lie scattered here
a hundred years,
    a hundred years
        and more.

In November, 1868, hostile Cheyenne warriors who had been plundering and killing in Kansas, were tracked to the Washita River village of the nominally peaceful Cheyenne Chief, Black Kettle, by Lieutenant Colonel George A. Custer and the Seventh Cavalry. In a dawn fight, Black Kettle, and many others were killed. The horse herd was also destroyed.

PHRENOLOGY

"We have no more heart..." CHIEF GIAN-NA-TAH

GENERAL CARLTON SHIPPED the head of Mangas Coloradas
to Washington in a jar. The body
was buried quickly before the bayonet wounds
could be found; before a court discovered
how soldiers stabbed their sleeping prisoner.
How goaded, chased, he ran, a startled antelope,
into the valley he loved and trusted.

"Shot trying to escape," they reported, then
cleaned their rifles, sharpened the axe.

The phrenologist's answer came back.
"A smart Indian. Brain bigger
than Daniel Webster's."

ACOMA PUEBLO

YOU COME here
climbing, breathless,
as you must to hill towns,
aloof above the ground,
eye to eye with hawks,

and what you find
is wind
winding
through the flutter and hush
of time.

You need this music,
for perched upon the rock
looking out and out
you see the hopelessness
of bodies and desire.

You touch the wind's taut wire,
permit it entry,
and the humming lifts you
lightly from your bones.

Released now,
at ease with wings and sky,
you taste the truth
of resurrection.

HORSES

I N THE RAIN, between Mexican Water
and Chinle Wash, where the earth
is the color of a faded rose
and where the wind has carved
the eye of an eagle into the bluff,
twelve gray horses were dancing.

The suddenness of storm,
the sweetness of water
after the long drought
possessed them.
They whirled and pranced
to thunder's drum,
heads high, nostrils red,
tails tossed by the wind.

There are moments that stay forever
in the labyrinth of heart and eye,
and so it is with this vision
of horses—a dream of arcs and angles
moving on the silk screen of rain.

SAN ILDEFONSO PUEBLO

UNDER THE TASSELS of elms
the old man polishes shells,
sifting through rainbows
and singing in time.

Like the ragged dog asleep
beside him, he has been waiting
for Spring, for warmth.
Soon he will place his pots to dry,
those realities he made the old way,
dreaming the shapes of earth,
the mica from secret places.

He will tell you
that only his grandmother
remembers the source
of that shining sand,
that he steals it from her
when she isn't watching,
which is often now.

He will tell you how he knows
that Spring will come again.
The elms are braiding their hair.
The blackbirds bend the branches down
dancing...
            in love.

FALSE GODS
(The San Simon Valley, 1993)

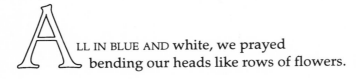 LL IN BLUE AND white, we prayed
bending our heads like rows of flowers.

God was on the altar, they told us,
and God was good. We believed, and yet

some skepticism writhed in me,
flawed bloom in that perfect garden.

I had too many questions, they said.
I had no faith. Love, alone, was not enough.

They are all dead now, those dark women
more flawed than I. Outraged, they lie

between plain boards, hands crossed,
eyes blank as stones.

Perhaps their words play back to them,
sift into their ears

with the slow evolution
of mountain into dust.

What's immortal? I demand of their ghosts.
Whose word choose above the rest?

No answer comes, nor punishment.
Hawks circle the blue air.
The escarpment shudders to an end
like afternoon.

Watching, I know what I have always known.
That everything is holy—rivers, rocks,
steppes of colored grass, the split second
before dawn comes screaming from sleep
and light lifts like a tabernacle against sky.

VANISHED ARIZONA
(For Martha Summerhayes)

MARTHA, YOUR Arizona
is gone but not vanished.
The desert that crept
into your bones is here,
the shadows, the river.

I've seen the Colorado
where you bathed
in the coolness of dawn,
the red-silt water
. feeding the banks,
the tossing reeds.

Did the small clam shells
entrance you?
Did you carry them home
in your hand, your pocket
for your child to wonder over?

Did you laugh,
you and your company
of women as you splashed,
sang, bathed the sweat
from your bodies?

I think so. Here on the shore
I hear your voices,
the happiness of women—
Indian, Mexican, White.

Here, the current sweeps away years
and I sing with you
of the land,
the desert,
of mountains that lift to the sky.

In 1908, Martha Summerhayes published her memoir, Vanished Arizona, *a classic, and one of the loveliest books written by an army officer's wife. The book has been reprinted by the University of Nebraska Press.*

IN YUMA PRISON

M ARIA
    Eulogia
      Teresa
        Elena

Kate
  Edie
    Georgie
      Isabella...

These were the women imprisoned
in cells ten feet by eight
dug into the bowels of earth
and barred.

Why? For adultery, assault,
writhing retributions for abuse.

One husband stabbed,
another with his back in shreds.
A brother with his head blown off.
An infant, newborn, thrown to the water.
Moses?
No.
Another proof of fallibility,
unwanted, unloved.

I think they were all unloved.
I think after days, months, years
madness took them,
prisoners before the act
and after;

that one after the other
they rose up screaming,
clutching knives, infants,
their own misused bodies

and stabbed their offenders
over
    and over
        and over again.

MEMENTOS

THE OLD COCOONS of moths are all
that decorate the trees
this season.

Even their mirrors, the creeks,
   are in retreat, cold shards
      broken in passing.

What's left of summer
   are these dark shrouds dangling
      over skeletons of weeds.

What's left lies buried
   deep as love or courage
      under stiff stems

under sky pale as dried flowers.
   Old lace laid carefully away
      waiting to live again.

LANDSCAPE WITH EMPTY BARN
(Park County, Montana)

NO FOOL BUILT this barn
with stone foundation
timbers thick as a man's arm,
a gambrel roof to let the snow
slide quickly down.

Whoever he was,
he must have been proud
to see it here
between the curve
of two green hills.

But he had no time to eulogize.
He bent his back against winds,
his head to the spring calves,
his hands to seed heads
dancing in the fields.

A practical man,
his dreams used good timber,
stamped themselves cleanly
on the flanks of hills,
the shoulders of sky.

ODD LOTS

ARCHIE KEEPS A MULE, a mare,
a yellow cat for company,
but a long time back
he kept a mountain lion
in a barrel.

He let her out for exercise,
his coon hounds ready
to run her up the windmill
if she tried for the hills.

"But it wasn't right," he says.
"She just lay there in the dark
and cried sometimes.
Besides, you can't talk to a lion.
There's nothing you can say
she don't already know."

WINTER LIGHT

I GATHER THEM:
cold stars
ashes of goldenrod
feline stems of sumac
thinking to preserve
pale, brittle beauty,

thinking that we,
each of us,
want everything
want all
all at once,

even seasons
even the vintage
from withered fruit.

CALDERA

TEN MILLION years ago
this mountain opened its jaws
and blew its head apart.

What remained was a bowl,
curving, indestructible.
Today I stand in it thinking
I am tired of pliancy,
of prayers for fortitude
wept in the night.

Have mercy…
    have mercy…

I can hear them,
the voices tolling guilt,
the women, bent,
who, drowning, cling
to paradise.

I think of mountains
and how the grama grass
moves in the wind,
curved seeds scattering.

I think of running into the caldera,
a pale horse, riderless.
Of moving across the yellow earth,
female, spilling out,
existing for myself.

THE RED
DRUM

LOST LAMBS

THEY STOP AT my blue gate,
   a young man and the girl
   he calls his wife,
   though I doubt it.
She's impermanent,
fragile-boned as tumbleweed.

She says they've lost a lamb,
looking at my dogs as she speaks.
I don't tell her that, alone,
it stands no chance,
that lions or coyotes and not my dogs
will find it, bring it down
bleating in moonlight.

Last summer another pair stopped here.
A small man and a woman with a devastated face.
They were looking for their son
who had disappeared.
They'd posted his picture everywhere—
the store, the post office,
on the rough surfaces of telephone poles.

I said nothing then, either,
simply wished them luck
and watched them drive away
across the heat-fired plain,
knowing that under the brilliance,
beneath the yellow grasses
the thin stems of trees
and cascading yucca flowers,
the heart of earth beats
like a red drum,

that every species in the world
lies buried beside the throbbing,
white bones shaken into dust.

DRIVING THE BORDER

COMING HOME at night alone
 on the dark road along the border,
  my only landmarks are the mountains,
  black on black,
and the road uncoiling like a whip.

It's not an easy journey.
Cattle wander out and stand
solid as boulders, dark as hills.
Mule deer leap and javelina
haunt the ditches.
Men, too. The runaways, the smugglers
savage as knives crouch in the weeds.
I know they're there. I sense them
and drive armed, locked in my metal shell.

I steer the white line,
bless the moon when it comes
running fence wires
and turning blank fields to snow.

I have tried to explain its brightness
to city friends in sealed houses.
I have described the leaves of trees
flicking like silverfish,
the lift of earth toward sky.

But something in cities defeats the moon—
other lights, perhaps, or the reality of fear.
My friends remain captive and do not answer
when I tell them how I open the window
and drive through waves of light
that startle like white water touching stone.

WATER SPOUTS

THEY SEEM SUCH simple things
these water spouts; graceful
as mist, pale-throated
as calla lilies.

I watch them without fear
as they spiral down the valley
trailing one long root,

and I ask why it is
that loveliness
is so often lethal,

why we never step away
but run forward to meet it—
men, women, our faith in our hands.

CUTTING CALVES

THROWING AND tying calves is hard work,
harder today with a forty-mile wind
and blowing sand stinging our faces.

Roberto ropes them. I grab diagonal legs
and drop the bawling bundles on their sides
for Beto to tie up with piggin' strings.

It's like a dance, a prescribed minuet,
each gesture meaningful though uncourtly,
and no accompaniment but wind,

the hollering of mothers and sons.
Beto draws his knife,
runs a horny finger up the glinting blade,

and with a sneer offers it to me,
handle first. It's a dare I can't refuse.
He wants to see me, the *gringa*, faint,

but he'll get no satisfaction.
I kneel beside a spotted calf
that's worn out from struggling

and lies terrified and still.
We look at each other,
he with frightened, iridescent eyes.

I tell myself, *This is what you do.*
What has always been done.
Then I take the sack and cut

quick as a surgeon, reach
for the testicles red as plums,
and cut again. I go on to the next,

refusing to think until I'm through
and the men with fierce eyes and moustaches
offer their hands, bow over bloody fingers.

The wind's in our faces the ten miles home,
and my horse trots like a jackhammer
leaving me breathless, light as tumbleweed in the saddle.

BUZZARDS

I HAVE ASKED where the buzzards go
in winter, but no one knows.
One day they are simply gone
leaving the sky wiped clean.

What I believe is that they follow plenty,
winging south to the jungles
where war and famine, pestilence
and greed make death commonplace;

where they can eat their fill,
warm their reptilian hearts
at equatorial fires,
follow the scent of the dying
for thousands and thousands of miles.

POMEGRANATES

I AM PICKING the fruits of Persia—
apricots, figs, pomegranates
red-muscled as hearts.

These are the transplants of history,
of Homer, Alexander, an oasis
called Babylon. This is the harvest,
this pulp the color of blood.

I reach and pluck,
an ancient act,
ancient as love or war
or the fall from paradise.

When the sweet spoils
drench my mouth
I stand, blessed by shadow,
wondering how we have come
so far from grace.

ALIENS

I SEE THEM, the small dark men
thin as birds, determined as earthworms.
Guided by seasons, they move north in lines
longer than imagination or belief,
a migration as surely as the birds they resemble.

They stop at my door
asking for work, for water,
and their eyes dart like tongues
around corners, searching for danger.

There is always danger.
It is a fact of their lives
like hunger and the roads
that burn through boots,
the heat that turns them old
before their time.

My water comes out of earth,
not mine to keep.
I give it freely.
It is all I have.
That and compassion
for such simple desperation,
reaching out year after year
for life, like every creature,
every flower
in the field.

FACADES

I TREAT THEM gently,
these little men
from Zacatecas, Juarez,
Chihuahua;
these laborers who
chop tumbleweeds,
dig ditches,
build the finest
of stone walls
and for nothing—
a bed, water, food,
what payment
I can summon.

Dear God! I have become
the patroness of souls,
hands, stomachs,
the repository of dreams.

They come and they come.
Jesus, Abel, Alfredo,
with hands that know horses,
that cradle the large heads
as if they are women,
with tongues that speak
softly, quickly
in a language I do not—
may never—
understand.

TRUCKSTOP: NEW MEXICO

THE WAITRESS behind the counter
has a face like old shoes —
chin jutting, her mouth
a crevasse of despair.

She wears stripes of blue eyeshadow
above frayed cheekbones,
has colored her hair with henna
then crimped it into disarray.

When I ask for water, she looks at me,
her blue mask a battle cry.
She is the warrior here,
I, the supplicant.

She knows the desert has flayed me,
that alkali dries from the inside
out. She has always known.
It is why she is here,

lost Magdalene.
Why she never looks out
and paints her bold face
without using a mirror.

SEEDS OF DESTRUCTION

IN THE MORNING a thousand moths
float on the surface of the trough,
fragile, transparent, doomed
to death by innocence.

So many!
So many wings
like ruffled fans,
old lace, striped scarves,
petals of blossom blown
into dark water.

They come together,
a delicate, common shroud,
and though I dip them out
they turn to dust
that gilds my fingers
and falls to earth
like shattered stars.

THE CAVES

ALL THESE YEARS I never saw the caves.
Perhaps the summer trees obscured the cliffs,
or sunlight angling into the canyon
made mockery of any opening but sky.

Today, with snow falling then blowing back—
a curtain of mist—the black holes
loomed a thousand feet above,
higher than cathedral doors.

It seemed the mountain had opened many mouths
and revealed its differences, and I, standing below,
my hand on its cold flesh, felt as we do
when the familiar turns alien,
when what is beloved exposes labyrinths
we dare not enter.

ASPENS

SEE HOW THE aspens march
  to the edge of the bluff,
    a bright fire blazing
  in the bell-like air.

Look your fill
for loveliness is the harbinger
of change. Look now
or go blind.
It is a dare,

a danger catching
at the throat.
The future's an abyss
unseen, uncharted, and though
you cry out in despair

you must take this moment.
Gather these golden, dancing things
and hold them close
though they flutter out of reach
and, falling, leave white branches bare.

Jornada Del Muerto

ALL YOUR LIFE you have moved
toward this solitude,
toward the heart
of desert country.

Red and roaring,
rocks rear around you,
while you curve your body
cup the steady fire
move through the forge
of heat and sand.

You gather yourself,
taut as a bow,
and face the wind.
After years of choices
you hear what the dazzle tells you,
and the teeth of mountains grinding down...

that endurance is the only necessary thing.

RAISON D'ETRE

THE DRAGONFLY was almost dead.
Glued, flightless, to algae,
it held with two black legs to life
and writhed and twisted,
each motion slower than the last

until I freed it,
took it on a twig,
and like a surgeon probing
through a lens
loosened wings from scum,
legs from slime.

The wings lay on my knee, transparent,
and the body, the six-inch enamel body,
turquoise, black, shaped for flying,
lay there still, as if with knowledge
that my hands were skilled.

But my hands are adept at nothing.
I cannot sew or play without an error.
Given a knife I cut myself and bleed.
Only in this act did I work surely,
willing the ability to soar and hover
back into that slender brilliance
holding to my knee.

Now I can say that once
I saved a dragonfly from drowning,
that it flew, flashing over the pond
and returned again and again
before melting into sky.

FAITH

THE BLACK COW
has come home to die.
For two days she has
blocked the road
with her body,
her patience.

"Water belly," they call
this affliction—
in other words,
death by drowning.

When I stop beside her
with some notion
of compassion,
she takes no notice.

And what, after all,
can I say
across the kingdoms
that divide us?

What hope give to her
who has none,
who has never had hope
or words, only gone on
year after year,
waking, sleeping,
giving birth
in the simplicity of total faith.

FLICKA

THE OLD MARE stands guard
over her feed box.
She lays back her ears,
shows her teeth,
pins me to the wall.

Broken hard,
she loves no one
but does what she is told
except at feeding time
when she demands what is hers.

There are many like her.

DOVE HUNTING

TO COOK THEM, first pluck,
  discard all
  but the breasts
  and grill quickly.

Doves are small.
Prepare at least four
per person, then
eat if you can.

As for me—
having year after year
shared a garden
with a nesting pair,
having rested in the shadows
of their wings—

I can neither shoot
nor eat
these sweet flutes—
these symbols
of lasting peace.

RECOVERY

NIGHT RECEDES slowly, in acts,
like a play. I can tell you this
having spent weeks of nights
by the window waiting for pain to ease,
for the sun to rise, for characters
to move down roads and bring the fields to life.

I have watched the sky
form into pools like those
the tide leaves behind.
Each clutches light
then overflows, spilling
tremulous dawn across dark earth
and into the room where,
little by little, the shapes
that guard me soften,
become table, lamp, plant
whose ghostly leaves
shadow the wall.

I shift in my chair—
the one I've slept in—
and curse my brittle bones,
the sorrel horse that, wanting freedom,
took the fence and left me behind.

Understanding comes slowly as day
and the discovery of hungers.
Freedom is both motion and morning—
the lure of terra-cotta hills,
the sun like a thousand oranges
pelting a hot blue sky.

RUNNING

I T WAS THE SUMMER I played horse all day,
prick-eared, quick as wind,
king of the tadpole pond and the orchard
where the apples lay dreaming.
It was the summer my father brought
the crippled boys to hike and play.

Drooling and shuffling, they crossed
the fields that I had crossed
at a gallop, a canter, a trot,
and they stood thinking hard
about how to climb fences.

I ran ahead, unnoticed by them,
shackled to disobedient bodies.
Or perhaps secretly they hated
the sound my hooves made,
the dust I raised and they swallowed
as they pushed through weeds on crooked feet.
Perhaps they hungered for the berries
I ate before they got there,
so nothing was left but thorns.

It is years since I've thought of them,
the mottled faces, the hands
that never connected to things.
It is years since I've remembered their eyes
that fastened on stones as if they were walls
to be scaled, lurched over,
that followed me from behind goldenrod
and split rail fences.
Years since I've thought of the sounds they made,
the noises that passed for laughter,
that jarred the trees and spurred me on,
neighing, shying away from shadows.

BEYOND THE
MERIDIAN

BEYOND THE HUNDREDTH MERIDIAN

THESE ARE THE dangerous hours.
The prairie twilight stretches out
like a blackbird's whistle
or the flight of moths
and a blue mist binds me,
hands and heart,
to earth.

I touch its green flanks,
its dark muscle
and think of women
big as mares or buffalo
who marked these grasses
with broad shoulders,
steady feet.

In their image I lie down
in the tasseled grass
in the music of larks
in the dangerous hours
and give my body over.

CHIRICAHUA AUTUMN

YOU WRITE THAT the aspens have turned to gold,
that the acorn gatherers have come
moving among oaks and filling baskets
with brown fruit.

Like the mallards that took wing
before you thought to watch their flight,
the pickers came and vanished,
leaving earth the way it was...

mountains
   valleys stretching blue
      aspens shaking golden tambourines.

AIR POWER

DO YOU SEE that field?
It belongs to no one.
The hawk that circles there
is the possessor,

knowing land and air,
the vole, the nest of lark,
the clear rust red of racer
slipping through pale grass.

He knows them,
sees them all at once,
dips dark wings and glides
the edges of his territory
needing no signature
but flight.

BALD EAGLE

THE WIND IS filled with temptations.
The sky blows blue
like glimpses of the wings
of startled jays
behind a culmination of trees.

Beyond fear,
too high for shadows,
the eagle drifts,
wing tips spread
like fingers in the wind.

Watching
I am weakened
by a need more fierce
than jealousy,
more awful
than desire
to share the silence
of the air,
to know myself
in solitude.

CHANGING

IT HAPPENS so suddenly...
the lifting of birds
the sweep of horses
out of cloud into sunlight.

You raise your arms,
begin to run
and when the wind
makes your breath its own

you realize you are divisible...
    into the tossing branch,
       the flowering birds,
           horses moving the wind.

WOMAN BESIDE THE LAKE

THE GEESE WITH undulant black necks have gone
   arrowing down the great flyway
   like the orioles that swayed in hanging baskets
   and sang the sun to sleep.

You have rolled up the rugs,
hidden the pillows from winter mice,
turned the key in the lock.

In air clear as a flask
you sit in the cove's palm
where water boatmen sculled in summer.
Goldenrod has replaced meadow rue,
and bows have turned to bone.

The dead pine, fox-red,
stands humming,
and leaves the bronzed purple of grackle wings
float out of reach
across the slow, still surface
of the autumn lake
like all the days of summer.

WOMAN PICKING APPLES

YOU HAVE HIDDEN your hair
in a scarf.
A sun-squint keeps your eyes
from burning,
sky-blue, fierce as flame.

The air is golden
with September dust,
brilliant
with the beating wings of wasps
until the height of noon
lays stillness on the leaves.

You will know
a moment of becoming,
absorb the way the field bursts
at the river edge,
stop, collect the hour
like fruit that quivers
on the palm.

You will remember
the pulse
within your throat,
the high arc of your arm,
and how you touched
the hovering transparency
of time.

Young Fisherman

Your pride lies at my feet.
Five trout
with golden scales
layered like fans.

Five dazzling bodies on the grass.
Your dreams
and all these lives
that flashed and leaped
and cut the air with light.

Your eyes snare me.
The knife
is cold,
the bodies
resist,
slip through my hands
as if through water.

Like this, you say.
You show me how
to grasp the tail,
ribbed, translucent,
still, as dying is.

IN THE SIERRAS

LIKE CASSANDRA beating
at the gates of Troy,
I look out a hundred miles
the taste of defeat
sharp in my throat.

Language is futile here
where the shapes of history
rise, sing, fall away like thunder.

Stricken, I reach for the small—
pebbles, grains of sand,
the grass, the poppies dancing.
These I can grasp,
arrange in lines,
conquer on paper.

These tangible lives that go on
beneath mountains
are all that succumb
to the hands of a lesser god.

AT THE GRAND CANYON

SILENCE...
    earth drops away
       in tiers, chasms,
          spirals of history.

Silence...
   filling a well
     I had not known
       was dry.

Silence...
   only the raven dares
     to steer into the wind
       and fly

small, small
   above the red wound
     that's simply space
       to a space-haunted eye.

A TIME TO PLOW

PAUL PLOW man,
  secured by my madness,
  has eaten, smoked,
  now sleeps against the wall
while I weave valleys
flicked over by birds.

Thud of hooves
swish of tails
beat of wings
continuo
  andante
earth released
by silver edge
in time for greening.

Among lichens
the plow man dreams
and I, alive from inside out,
ride soundless in the bowl
of the ringing field.

LIVING WITH A WINDMILL

FIRST YOU MUST adjust it—
not you but someone brave enough
to climb the narrow stairs,
maneuver underneath
the whirling blades.

Set the brakes
then loosen them,
hang nimbly
from the wooden walk,
one arm free
the other straining,
overworked.

The poetry here is balance,
the language of the body
tuned to height
and the whimsy of weather.

Words come later
like the gush of water
from underground,
like the steady hum
of rods, pump,
the great spinning wheel
in harmony,
stealing the wind.

THE GREAT PLAINS

"A clover and one bee..."

EVERY TIME I cross these plains
I think of Emily Dickinson.
Not kindly, either. This is not
a poem of praise. It is a first.

We worship around the Belle
as iconoclasts around a fatted calf,
fearful of retribution from feminists,
professors of literature, little ladies
in lace collars who never saw the prairie
but who flutter over clovers and bees.

There is more to the plains
than one zany princess could grasp.
Sweep of wind, grass hugging black earth,
a sky so large it challenges.
Cut-banks, coulees, buffalo humped
on a horizon that keeps drawing away.
You feel it the length of your body.
You grow to meet it.
There's room to expand beyond
white bedrooms and black ovens
built to bake currant cake.

What do those things have to do with magnificence?

What did those fleshy lips in that spoiled face
know about joy? A shout into the mouth
of a wind so long it meets itself?
About light like a rain of glass?
About dancing unencumbered by the long skirts
of misplaced chastity?

So I think about her when I roll down the windows
and gulp the scented air. When I leave the car
and run through wild roses
and through the green arms of corn.

THE PERSEID METEORS

W E HAVE COME to watch the meteors
detach themselves from sky
and run the night
swift as fire.

We reach for them
wishing to be stars.
We whisper
the uninhabited places.

They speak our dreams...
the touch
the long journey
the open throat of sky
falling....

PUEBLO BOWL

THIS MORNING the bowl from Zia,
   earth-tawny, pale as apricots,
quickens on the sill
and gathers light.

It is made for holding,
broad, curved, the color
of your skin in summer.

The cool clay warms
and I say, *This is how it was...*

this is how I held your face
   ripe fruit
      vessel of sweet water.

BLUE SKY WITH SUNFLOWERS

YOU FIGHT IT. Your own voice
that covets sunflowers
streaming in the light
like a million butterflies.

Pick! Take all of them! it tells you,
greedy for windy splendor.
But who has room to keep a field,
a net to trap the whole September sky?

Instead you memorize the yellow flight,
then, bending, cup your hands
around the gaudy faces
of impossible desire.

MILKING

WE GO TO BRING the cows home,
and they come in their hang-bellied trot,
watching us with the round-eyed wariness
of half wild things.

You laughed when I asked
to learn to milk.
My hands would freeze
to the udders in winter, you said.
The cows would kick,
butt me against board walls,
switch my face with filthy tails.

Still, I had to know
for a reason not apparent.
It is a secret thing,
the giving of milk.
A mystery
like love and birth,
the pouring forth
of what was taken.

DEFENDING THE CREEK

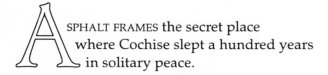 SPHALT FRAMES the secret place
where Cochise slept a hundred years
in solitary peace.

Soon these mountains,
cherished by Geronimo
by red-sleeved Mangas
and the rest who love
the rock-bound loneliness,
will be given to the world.

An amphitheater here,
a ski lodge in the lion's
last retreat,
a campground for those
in metal shells who peek
at wilderness.

I've witnessed other murders.
Seen factories where herons
nested in the tops of trees,
a freeway where a flock
of mallards fed and chicory
reflected summer sky.

I've seen the small worlds
handed to the large
in the name of progress
and the public good.
I've watched the darkening
of wild-eyed light,
walked the devastated earth
and wept.

But tears are useless now.
Bring on an army armed with words,
in love with history;
forceful as the wind,
entrenched as deeply
as the native grass
and passionate.

Above all, passion,
that fuel to the spark of love,
that wise seed,
that flaming ocotillo flower.

ABOUT THE AUTHOR

JANE CANDIA COLEMAN is the recipient of two Western Heritage Awards from the National Cowboy Hall of Fame—for her first volume of poetry, *No Roof But Sky*, and for her first collection of short fiction, *Stories From Mesa Country*. She was also awarded a Spur Award for short fiction from Western Writers of America. Her first novel, *Doc Holliday's Woman*, is forthcoming from Warner Books.

Born in Pittsburgh, Pennsylvania, but hungering even as a child for the West, she made her first trip there in 1965 and moved to a ranch in Cochise County, Arizona, in 1986.

Of *The Red Drum*, she writes… "Living close to the land, the High Desert of the Southwest, I have come to believe in the inherent justice of the natural world.

"While we often view it as a joyous, spiritual partner that beckons us to a kind of mystical union, nature can be violent, even cruel as well as beautiful. The earth belongs to itself, governs itself, much as we would like to think otherwise. The poems in *The Red Drum* attempt to deal with both the reality of nature and our need for its beauty as inspiration.

"I love this earth, and I give thanks for it daily, but my love is shaped by respect for a rightness, a balance I cannot change nor truly be part of.

"As Charley Russell said about a potential buyer who wanted him to paint out the blood and violence in his picture, 'Tell her that's the way it was!' And that's the way it still is."

Jane Candia Coleman
Cochise County, Arizona
Near Rodeo, New Mexico
September 1994

*The text is composed in
eleven-point Adobe Palatino.
Display type is also Adobe Palatino.
The dropped display initials
are modified Caxton Roman Light Italic.
This book is printed on
sixty-pound Glatfelter Supple Opaque
acid-free, recycled paper
by Thomson-Shore.*